W9-ABY-984

COOL
Eating

HEALTHY & FUN WAYS TO EAT RIGHT

Alex Kuskowski

A Division of ABDO

ABDO
Publishing Company

visit us at www.abdopublishing.com

Published by ABDO Publishing Company, a division of ABDO, P.O. Box 398166, Minneapolis, Minnesota 55439. Copyright © 2013 by Abdo Consulting Group, Inc. International copyrights reserved in all countries. No part of this book may be reproduced in any form without written permission from the publisher. Checkerboard Library™ is a trademark and logo of ABDO Publishing Company.

Printed in the United States of America, North Mankato, Minnesota
062012
092012

 PRINTED ON RECYCLED PAPER

Design and Production: Mighty Media, Inc.
Series Editor: Liz Salzmann
Photo Credits: Colleen Dolphin, Shutterstock

The following manufacturers/names appearing in this book are trademarks: Clear Value®, Marukan®, McCormick®, Pillsbury®, Reynolds®, Roundy's®, Target®, Thai Kitchen®

Library of Congress Cataloging-in-Publication Data

Kuskowski, Alex.
 Cool eating : healthy & fun ways to eat right / Alex Kuskowski.
    p. cm. -- (Cool health and fitness)
 Audience: 8-12
 Includes index.
 ISBN 978-1-61783-426-4
 1. Nutrition--Juvenile literature. 2. Health--Juvenile literature. I. Title.
 RA784.K885 2013
 613.2--dc23
                              2012010052

CONTENTS

THINK FOOD!

It's time to take charge of your eating. Eating healthy is good for your body and your brain. You'll feel faster and stronger and have more energy. Once you get started eating healthy you'll wonder why you weren't doing it all along!

You don't have to give up your favorite foods to eat right. Being healthy begins with eating a balanced diet. Make sure to eat fruits and veggies along with your favorite foods. And how much you eat is as important as what you eat. See page 7 for healthy portion sizes for different foods.

Permission & Safety

- Always get **permission** before cooking at home.
- If you do something by yourself, make sure you do it safely.
- Ask for help when necessary.
- Be careful when using sharp objects.
- Make sure you're wearing the **appropriate** gear.

Be Prepared

- Read the entire activity before you begin.
- Make sure you have all the tools and materials listed.
- Do you have enough time to complete the activity?
- Keep your work area clean and organized.
- Follow the directions.
- Clean up any mess you make.

Hot and Sharp!

Be especially careful using hot or sharp things while cooking. When you use the oven, stove, or knives, make sure an adult is nearby to help if needed.

EATIN' RIGHT

There are a lot of things you can do to eat right. One of the best is to make your own healthy food. When you make a meal, be sure to include fruits, veggies, and whole grains. They are the three main food groups your body needs most.

Every dish is a chance for you to get creative. Try a new type of healthy food, or add fruits and veggies to your favorite dishes. Have a health food cook-off with your friends. Most of all, have fun with your food!

Food Rules!

X Don't skip any meals. Try to eat your meals at about the same time each day.

X Use portion control. See the page 7 for suggestions.

X Eat slowly to help your body recognize when it is full.

X Exercise to keep your **metabolism** going.

SERVING SIZES

VEGGIES

2 to 3 servings per day
- 1 cup of vegetable juice
- 1 cup of raw or cooked vegetables
- 2 cups of leafy greens

FRUITS

1 to 2 servings per day
- 1 cup of fresh fruit
- ½ cup of dried fruit

PROTEINS

5 servings per day
- 1 ounce of meat or fish
- 1 egg
- ¼ cup cooked beans
- 1 tablespoon peanut butter

WHOLE GRAINS

5 to 6 servings per day
- 1 slice of bread
- 1 cup of **cereal**
- ½ cup of rice or pasta

DAIRY

3 servings per day
- 1 cup of milk or yogurt
- 1 slice of cheese

MAKE TIME TO EAT RIGHT!

AROUND THE HOUSE (INSIDE)

One secret to eating healthy is keeping tasty and **nutritious** foods in your house. Stock your kitchen with healthy snacks such as fresh fruit, crunchy veggies, and creamy yogurt.

PACKING A SNACK

Instead of potato chips or cookies, choose a healthy treat. Make a trail mix with nuts and dried fruit. It's healthy and **delicious**! And you can take it with you anywhere.

AROUND THE HOUSE (OUTSIDE)

One of the best ways to get fresh fruits and vegetables is to grow your own. Plant a garden in your back yard. Ask an adult for help getting started.

PLUGGED IN

Most kids use computers for talking to friends and doing homework. You can use your computer to find new recipes or cooking tips! Try healthy recipes you find online.

ON THE ROAD

On car rides, especially road trips, it can be tough to eat healthy. Try bringing healthy **sandwiches** and snacks along. You'll save money and avoid unhealthy fast food.

AT SCHOOL

Eating right can be hard at school. Try packing a healthy lunch to bring with you. If you get lunch in the cafeteria, make healthy choices. Ask for extra veggies and avoid fried foods.

WITH FRIENDS

Eat healthy with your friends. Doing it together makes it even easier to eat right. And cooking healthy foods with friends can be a lot of fun!

COOL COOKING BASICS

STIR

Stir means to mix ingredients together, usually with a large spoon.

DRAIN

Drain means to remove liquid using a strainer or colander.

GRATE

Grate means to shred something into small pieces using a grater.

SLICE

Slice means to cut food into pieces of the same thickness.

BOIL

Boil means to heat liquid until it begins to bubble.

DICE

Dice means to cut something into small squares with a knife.

SUPPLIES

Here are some of the things that you'll need to get started!

baking sheet

colander

cutting board

ice-pop molds

large pot

measuring cups & spoons

mixing bowls

mixing spoon

non-stick pan

nori mat

parchment paper

pizza pan

plastic wrap

small pot

spatula

whisk

THE GOODS

Here is some of the food that you'll need to get started!

almond extract

avocados

bell peppers

coconut milk

edamame

granola

grated cheddar cheese

green onions

nori seaweed wrap

red pepper flakes

refrigerated sugar-
cookie dough

rice vinegar

soy sauce

sushi rice

taco seasoning

whole wheat pasta

Juicy Frushi

Fun fruit fusion!

WHAT YOU NEED

- 1 cup sushi rice
- ¼ cup of sugar
- ½ cup coconut milk
- ½ teaspoon of salt
- 6 ounces vanilla yogurt
- 2 strawberries, sliced
- 1 orange
- measuring cups
- measuring spoons
- small pot
- mixing bowl
- mixing spoon
- platter
- knife

1 Put 1 cup of water and the rice in a small pot over high heat. When it boils, cover the pot and turn the heat to low. Cook for 20 minutes.

2 Put the rice in a mixing bowl. Add the sugar, coconut milk, and salt. Stir well. Let it cool.

3 Divide the rice mixture into 10 equal portions. Shape each portion into a ball.

4 Put 1 teaspoon of yogurt on each rice ball. Top each ball with a strawberry or orange slice.

Edamame Beans

A super side dish!

1 pound edamame
1 teaspoon sea salt
measuring cups & spoons
large pot
colander
paper towel

1. Heat 3 cups of water in a large pot on high heat. When the water boils, add the edamame. Cook 10 minutes.

2. Drain the edamame in a colander. Pat it dry with a paper towel. Sprinkle salt over the edamame.

3. To eat, hold the stem of a pod and slide the beans out with your teeth.

Veggie Sushi Rockin' Roll

Roll that rice!

WHAT YOU NEED

- 1 cup sushi rice
- 1 tablespoon rice vinegar
- nori seaweed wrap
- ⅓ cup carrots, grated
- ⅓ cup avocado, sliced
- ⅓ cup bell pepper, sliced
- measuring cups & spoons
- small pot
- mixing bowl
- mixing spoon
- nori mat
- sharp knife
- cutting board

1 Put the rice and 2 cups water in a small pot over high heat. When it boils, cover the pot and turn the heat to low. Cook for 20 minutes.

2 Put the rice in a mixing bowl. Add the rice vinegar. Stir well. Let it cool.

3 Lay out the nori mat so the bamboo sticks are **horizontal**. Lay the nori seaweed wrap on it with the shiny side down. Spread the rice over the wrap. Leave 1 inch (2.5 cm) of the wrap uncovered at the bottom, and 1½ inches (3.8 cm) uncovered at the top.

4 Lay the vegetables in a line across the middle of the rice. Dip your fingers in a small bowl of water. Wet the top and bottom edges of the wrap.

5 Starting at the bottom, fold the mat over the vegetables. Tuck the edge of the seaweed wrap in. Keep rolling until the wrap is rolled up in a tube. Press down on the mat to make the roll stick.

6 Put the roll on a cutting board. Slice it into 2-inch (5 cm) pieces.

Sugar & Spice Nuts-To-Go

 A tasty traveling treat!

WHAT YOU NEED

- 1 cup walnuts
- 1 cup pecan halves
- 1 tablespoon honey
- 2 teaspoons olive oil
- 2 tablespoons sugar
- 1 teaspoon sea salt
- ½ teaspoon cinnamon
- ½ teaspoon ground cumin
- ⅛ teaspoon cayenne pepper
- baking sheet
- parchment paper
- measuring cups & spoons
- small pot
- mixing spoon

makes 4 servings

1 Cover the baking sheet with parchment paper. Set it aside.

2 Put the walnuts, pecans, honey, oil, and 2 tablespoons water in a small pot over medium heat. Stir to coat the nuts.

3 After 2 minutes, add the sugar, salt, cinnamon, cumin, and cayenne pepper. Stir constantly for 3 minutes.

4 Spread the nuts on the baking sheet. Let them cool completely before snacking.

TIP: Bring a napkin along to clean your hands after!

Fruity Frozen Yogurt Pops

Take a computer break with this treat!

WHAT YOU NEED

- 2 cups plain yogurt
- ⅓ cup blueberries
- ⅓ cup granola
- ⅓ cup strawberry preserves
- measuring cups
- 2 medium bowls
- spoon
- ice-pop molds

1 Put 1 cup of yogurt in each of the two medium bowls.

2 Add the blueberries and granola to one bowl. Add the strawberry preserves to the other bowl. Stir both bowls well.

3 Fill each ice pop mold halfway with the strawberry preserve and yogurt mixture.

4 Then fill the rest of each mold up with the blueberry, granola, and yogurt mixture.

5 Insert the ice-pop sticks and freeze for 5 hours. To remove the yogurt pops, run warm water over the molds. This will loosen the pops.

Peanutty Pasta

The perfect pasta for lunch!

WHAT YOU NEED

- measuring cups & spoons
- large pot
- colander
- microwave-safe bowl
- plastic wrap
- fork
- mixing bowl
- sharp knife
- whisk

- cutting board
- mixing spoon
- hot pad
- ⅛ teaspoon salt
- 3 cups whole-wheat pasta
- 1 pound frozen broccoli

- 1 red bell pepper, chopped
- 2 tablespoons vegetable oil
- ¼ cup rice vinegar
- ¼ cup creamy peanut butter
- 2 tablespoons soy sauce
- ¼ teaspoon red pepper flakes
- 1 cup green onions, sliced
- ½ cup of peanuts, chopped

1   Put the salt and 6 cups of water in the large pot over high heat. When it boils, add the pasta. Cook according to the instructions on the pasta box. Drain the pasta in a colander. Set the pasta aside.

2   Put the broccoli and red pepper in a microwave-safe bowl. Cover with plastic wrap. Poke holes in the plastic with a fork.

3   Microwave on high for 4 to 5 minutes, or until broccoli is bright green. Use a hot pad to take the bowl out of the microwave.

4   Put the oil, vinegar, peanut butter, soy sauce, and red pepper flakes in a mixing bowl. Stir with a whisk.

5   Add the pasta, broccoli, red pepper, onions, and peanuts. Stir with a mixing spoon.

6   Take 1 cup of Peanutty Pasta to school for a healthy lunch!

Walking Tacos

Perfect for any party!

WHAT YOU NEED

- 1 pound ground beef
- 1 can of black beans
- 1 package taco seasoning
- 6 small bags of Doritos
- 3 cups grated cheddar cheese
- 3 tomatoes, diced
- 3 avocados, diced
- ½ cup sour cream
- colander
- mixing bowls
- non-stick pan
- spatula
- measuring cups
- small serving bowls
- scissors
- spoons
- sharp knife
- cutting board

makes 6 servings

1 Drain the can of black beans in the colander. Rinse the beans with cool water. Put them in a bowl and set aside.

2 Preheat the non-stick pan for one minute. Put in the ground beef. Stir with a spatula. Cook for 6 minutes or until the meat is light brown.

3 Stir in the beans and taco seasoning. Cook for 2 more minutes. Put the meat mixture in a bowl and let it cool. Put the cheese, tomatoes, avocados, and sour cream in small serving bowls.

4 To serve, give everyone a bag of chips. Have them gently crush the chips. When the chips are in small pieces, cut off the tops of the bags.

5 Let everyone add as much of each topping to their bags as they want. Then use spoons to eat the walking tacos right out of the bags!

TIP: When cooking the meat, make sure it all turns brown. Do not eat any meat that is still pink.

Fruit Pizza

Fantastically fruity!

what you need

- 18-ounce package refrigerated sugar-cookie dough
- 8 ounces vanilla yogurt
- ⅓ cup sugar
- ¼ teaspoon almond extract
- ¼ teaspoon vanilla extract

- 1 cup bananas, sliced
- 2 cups strawberries, sliced
- 1 cup blueberries
- ½ cup mandarin orange slices
- 1 kiwi, peeled and sliced
- sharp knife

- cutting board
- pizza pan
- measuring cups & spoons
- medium mixing bowl
- mixing spoon
- spatula

1   Preheat the oven to 350 degrees. Slice the cookie dough into thin circles.

2   Place the slices of dough in one layer on the pizza pan. Press the edges of the slices together.

3   Put the cookie dough in the oven for 10 minutes. Take it out and let it cool completely.

4   Put the yogurt, sugar, almond extract, and vanilla extract in a medium mixing bowl. Stir well.

5   Spread the yogurt mixture over the cookie crust.

6   Arrange the fruit slices on top of the yogurt. Get creative with your design!

TIP: Try making this pizza with different kinds of fruit. See which you like best!

Health Journal

Try keeping a health and fitness journal! Write down the foods you eat. Record what you have for breakfast, lunch, and dinner. Make sure to include snacks and drinks too. This makes it easy to look back and see how you are eating healthy. It could also show you where there's room for improvement. Decorate your journal to show your personal style!

Glossary

appropriate – suitable, fitting, or proper for a specific occasion.

cereal – a breakfast food usually made from grain and eaten with milk.

delicious – very pleasing to taste or smell.

horizontal – in the same direction as the ground, or side-to-side.

metabolism – the process the body uses to turn food into energy.

nutritious – good for people to eat.

permission – when a person in charge says it's okay to do something.

sandwich – two pieces of bread with a filling, such as meat, cheese, or peanut butter, between them.

web sites

To learn more about health and fitness for kids, visit ABDO Publishing Company online at www.abdopublishing.com. Web sites about ways for kids to stay fit and healthy are featured on our Book Links page. These links are routinely monitored and updated to provide the most current information available.

Index